WALTZING
ON
WATER

ALSO AVAILABLE IN LAUREL-LEAF BOOKS:

DEAR BILL, REMEMBER ME? AND OTHER STORIES,
Norma Fox Mazer
SUMMER GIRLS, LOVE BOYS AND OTHER STORIES,
Norma Fox Mazer
SOMEONE TO LOVE, *Norma Fox Mazer*
I, TRISSY, *Norma Fox Mazer*
UP IN SETH'S ROOM, *Norma Fox Mazer*
SATURDAY, THE TWELFTH OF OCTOBER,
Norma Fox Mazer
A FIGURE OF SPEECH, *Norma Fox Mazer*

WALTZING
— ON —
WATER

POETRY BY WOMEN

Edited by
Norma Fox Mazer
and
Marjorie Lewis

LAUREL-LEAF BOOKS bring together under a single imprint outstanding works of fiction and nonfiction particularly suitable for young adult readers, both in and out of the classroom. Charles F. Reasoner, Professor Emeritus of Children's Literature and Reading, New York University, is consultant to this series.

Published by
Dell Publishing
a division of
Bantam Doubleday Dell Publishing Group, Inc.
666 Fifth Avenue
New York, New York 10103

ISBN: 0-440-20257-4

Printed in the United States of America

February 1989

10 9 8 7 6 5 4 3 2

KRI

Contents

Introduction

III. with clown hats on . . .
                     love

VI.   magic to mix with time . . .

                            growing old

For my daughters:
  Vicki and Laurie
       M.L.

And for mine:
  Anne, Susan, and Gina
       N.F.M.

Introduction

These poems are about the shared experiences of women.

Here are the voices of women poets—voices stripped of falsity, open to humor, love, terror.

Give yourself to the poems. Read them aloud. Listen to their music. Feel their passion. The poets write about women's lives as children, as lovers, as friends, wives, mothers, and daughters. In these poems, you will find truths you never knew before. Or, perhaps, always knew but never in quite so magical a way.

In an image, a phrase, a stanza, with a handful of words, the poets—those blessed, mad, sensible women—say for us what we cannot say for ourselves.

Here, those captivating voices speak of the danger and the beauty of "waltzing on water."

Norma Fox Mazer
Marjorie Lewis

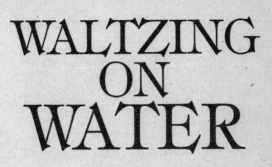

WALTZING
ON
WATER

I

I live on the
ceiling now . . .
         being young

THE GIRL IN THE GARDEN

A clearing in a dark garden or a small light patch
among black leaves. There I am, four years old,
mistress of celestial and red birds. I speak
to the most beautiful.
"I will give you to someone."
"How do you know I will be pleasing?" it asks.
"I will give you as a present," I say.
"You will never have anyone to give a bird to,"
says the bird.

ALEJANDRA PIZARNIK

*(translated from the Spanish
by Alina Rivero)*

CHILDHOOD

I used to lie on my back, imagining
A reverse house on the ceiling of my house
Where I could walk around in empty rooms
All by myself. There was no furniture
Up there, only a glass globe in the floor,
And knee-high barriers at every door.
The low silled windows opened on blue air.
Nothing hung in the closet; even the kitchen
Seemed immaculate, a place for thought.
I liked to walk across the swirling plaster
Into the parts of the house I couldn't see.
The hum from the other house, now my ceiling,
Reached me only faintly. I'd look up
To find my brothers watching old cartoons,
Or my mother vacuuming the ugly carpet.
I'd stare amazed at unmade beds, the clutter,
Shoes, half-dressed dolls, the telephone,
Then return dizzily to my perfect floorplan
Where I never spoke or listened to anyone.

I must have turned down the wrong hall,
Or opened a door that locked shut behind me,
For I live on the ceiling now, not the floor.
This is my house, room after empty room.
How do I ever get back to the real house
Where my sisters spill milk, my father calls,
And I am at the table, eating cereal?
I fill my white rooms with furniture,
Hang curtains over the piercing blue outside.
I lie on my back. I strive to look down.
The ceiling is higher than it used to be,
The floor so far away I can't determine
Which room I'm in, which year, which life.

MAURA STANTON

TO A DARK GIRL

I love you for your brownness
And the rounded darkness of your breast.
I love you for the breaking sadness in your voice
And shadows where your wayward eye-lids rest.

Something of old forgotten queens
Lurks in the lithe abandon of your walk
And something of the shackled slave
Sobs in the rhythm of your talk.

Oh, little brown girl, born for sorrow's mate,
Keep all you have of queenliness,
Forgetting that you once were slave,
And let your full lips laugh at Fate!

GWENDOLYN B. BENNETT

I AM ROSE

I am Rose my eyes are blue
I am Rose and who are you?
I am Rose and when I sing
I am Rose like anything.

GERTRUDE STEIN

CHARLOTTE'S WEB

I am sitting on the dock,
my mother is reading to me.
I am five
and cannot read.
It is the summer
I killed leeches,
curling them up with salt.
It is the summer
I almost drowned,
the summer I first stepped out of my body,
my hand touching a bolt of wool
in the Hudson's Bay store
while my brother buys a china teacup.
I cannot tell where my hand stops
and the fabric begins.
From across the room I am touching
the pale English downs
of the cup's landscape.

My mother is next to me,
holding the fabric she will buy.
I have entered other objects.
I want to ask if she knows
what I mean.
Suddenly the current snaps off.
I am not beating my way through the wool fiber,
I am not imprinted on the cup my brother is
    holding.

I left my skin and entered
several yards of red wool
but I am definitely back.
I am inside.
I can be removed from the Hudson's Bay store
without pain.

We are on the dock.
My mother reads
Charlotte's Web and stops
when I cry.
"Darling! Don't cry!"
"Keep reading, keep reading," I sob.
The voice starts up again
dry as hazelnuts,
slow voice that doesn't try to get away,
voice that does what I want,
softly bringing the story I love,
voice with more ocean than the ocean that laps
    near us,
voice, woman who cries for the death of a spider
    too.
Mother! We are on the dock,
rising and falling with fiction.

PATRICIA HAMPL

LIDDY'S ORANGE

The rind lies on the table where Liddy has left it
torn into pieces the size of petals and
curved like petals, rayed out like a
full-blown rose – one touch will make it come
    apart.
The lining of the rind is wet and chalky as
Devonshire cream, rich as the glaucous
lining of a boiled egg, all that protein
cupped in the ripped shell. And the navel,
torn out carefully,
lies there like a fat gold
bouquet, and the scar of the stem, picked out
with her nails, and still attached to the white
thorn of the central integument,
lies on the careful heap, a tool laid
down at the end of a ceremony.
All here speaks of ceremony:
the sheen of acrid juice, which is all that is
left of the flesh, the pieces lying in
profound order like natural order,
as if this simply happened, the way her
life at 13 looks like something that's just
happening, unless you see her
standing over it, delicately clawing it open.

SHARON OLDS

SUMMERS AGO
for Edith Sitwell

The ferryman fairied us out to sea
Gold gold gold sang the apple-tree

Children I told you I tell you our sun was a hail
    of gold!
I say that sun stoned, that sun stormed our
    tranquil, our blue bay
bellsweet saltfresh water (bluer than tongue-can-
    tell, daughter)
and dazed us, darlings, and dazzled us, I say that
    sun crazed
(that sun clove) our serene as ceramic selves and
    our noon-glazed cove,
and children all that grew wild by the wonderful
    water shot tall
as tomorrow, reeds suddenly shockingly green
    had sprouted like sorrow
and crimson explosions of roses arose in that
    flurry of Danaean glory
while at night we did swoon ah we swanned to a
    silverer moonlight than listen or lute,
we trysted in gondolas blown from glass and
    kissed in fluted Venetian bliss.

Sister and brother I your mother
Once was a girl in skirling weather
Though summer and swan must alter, falter,
I waltzed on the water once, son and daughter.

ISABELLA GARDNER

CHRONICLE

I was born the year of the loon
in a great commotion. My mother –
who used to pack $500 cash
in the shoulders of her fur gambling coat,
who had always considered herself
the family's "First Son" –
took one look at me
and lit out again
for a vacation to Sumatra.
Her brother purchased my baby clothes;
I've seen them, little clown suits
of silk and color.

Each day
my Chinese grandmother bathed me
with elaboration in an iron tub;
amahs waiting in lines
with sterilized water and towels
clucked and smiled
and rushed about the tall stone room
in tiny slippers.

After my grandfather
accustomed himself
to this betrayal by First Son,
he would take me in his arms,
walk with me
by the plum trees, cherries, persimmons;
he showed me the stiff robes
of my ancestors and their drafty hall,
the long beards of his learned old friends,
and his crickets.

Grandfather talked to me, taught me.
At two months, my mother tells me,
I could sniff for flowers,
stab my small hands upwards to moon.
Even today I get proud
when I remember
this all took place in Chinese.

MEI-MEI BERSSENBRUGGE

WORKING AROUND WORDS

Each summer they take an eyedropper
and squeeze green liquid into the lake.
I have never seen them, but Leonard,
who knows everything, has.
He says they row out to the middle
late at night, then lower the medicine
over the side of the boat.

It's done in a moment.
The next day the lake is yellow
and you will not let me swim in it.
You say my toes will turn black,
which is also what will happen if I lie.

Leonard has made me a promise
without crossing his fingers.
When I am thirteen
we will wait behind the trees
and watch them make the lake clean,
and before that, yellow.

PATRICIA FAREWELL

LIGHT YEARS

Didn't I have the name picked out
for my eventual stardom?
I practiced signing autographs

at seven. I knew I'd rise
above the dust motes when my mother
handed me the chamois and the Pledge.

I wouldn't have time to bother
matching napkins to Melmac plates,
even if there's something strangely

pretty in golden fleurs-de-lys
repeating over embossed tissue
paper, devised just to throw away.

What difference whether I folded
them so that all the ends met?
Their pattern more regular

and predictable than the stars,
the stars far away and cold
as I longed to be.

BARBARA ELOVIC

SPRING

When I was
thirteen I
believed that
the mailman
had sperm on
his hands and
if he touched
me I would
be pregnant
if he brushed
against me
in the hall
from my pores would sprout twigs branches
   leaves
buds blossoms unfurling I'd be an apple
tree in my white wedding dress swelling
the room until flowers exploded into the street
and rose up filling the sky blowsy with
         fruit to come

RUTH WHITMAN

GOOD-BYE TO
NEVER-NEVER LAND

Winnie-the-Pooh lives in the magic
   forest now,
and Raggedy Ann doesn't talk to Andy
   when I leave the room.
Monsters have abandoned their lair
   beneath my bed;
the gates to Oz and the Emerald City
   have been closed.
Monkey sits on the toy box and smiles,
   though he won't talk to me
as he did when I was afraid of the dark,
   and his companion Fee-Fee
can't find the red ribbon for his neck.
The Pink Elephant doesn't roam the
   mall in Fort Fatso; the Green Turtle
   is blue and has shrunk,
and I cannot crawl beneath him to find
   the magic places
where my friends and I used to live.

LEE ANN RORIPAUGH

II

green stars for eyes . . .
friendship

BEST FRIEND

Stella
appropriately
is fond of
astronomy
takes photographs
of starfish,
and has green stars
for eyes
at home in skies
where tigers walk
on clouds.

LILLIAN MORRISON

EMIGRATION

There are always, in each of us,
these two: the one who stays,
the one who goes away –
Charlotte, who stayed in the rectory
and helped her sisters die in England;
Mary Taylor, who went off to Australia
and set up shop with a woman friend.
"Charlotte," Mary said to her, "you are all
like potatoes growing in the dark."
And Charlotte got a plaque in Westminster
Abbey; Mary we get a glimpse of
for a moment, waving her kerchief
on the packet boat, and disappearing.
No pseudonym for her, and nothing
left behind, no trace
but a wide wake closing.

Charlotte stayed, and paid and paid –
the little governess with the ungovernable
heart, that she put on the altar.
She paid the long indemnity of all
who work for what will never wish them well,
who never set a limit to what's owed
and cannot risk foreclosure. So London
gave her fame, though it could never
sit comfortably with her at dinner –
how intensity palls when it is
plain and small and has no fortune.

When she died with her unborn child
the stars turned east
to shine in the gum trees of Australia,
watching over what has bypassed evolution,
where Mary Taylor lived
to a great old age, Charlotte's letters in a box
beside her bed, to keep her anger hot.

God bless us everyone until we sicken,
until the soul is like a little child
stricken in its corner by the wall; so there is
one who always sits there under lamplight
writing, staying on, and one
who walks the strange hills of Australia,
far too defiant of convention for the novels
drawn daily from the pen's "if only" –
if only Emily had lived,
if only they'd had money, if only
there had been a man who'd loved
    them truly . . .
while all the time there had been
Mary Taylor, whom no one would remember
except she had a famous friend named Charlotte
with whom she was so loving-angry, who
    up and left
to be a woman in that godforsaken outpost past
the reach of fantasy, or fiction.

ELEANOR WILNER

FOR JAN, IN BAR MARIA

Though it's true we were young girls when we
    met,
We have been friends for twenty-five years.
But we still swim strongly, run up the hill from
    the beach without getting too winded.
Here we idle in Ischia, a world away from our
    birthplace –
That colorless town! – drinking together, sisters
    of summer.
Now we like to have groups of young men
    gathered around us.
We are trivial-hearted. We don't want to die any
    more.

Remember, fifteen years ago, in our twin
    pinafores
We danced on the boards of the ferry dock at
    Mukilteo
Mad as yearling mares in the full moon?
Here in the morning moonlight we climbed on a
    workman's cart
And three young men, shouting and laughing,
    dragged it up through the streets of the village.
It is said we have shocked the people of Forio.
They call us Janna and Carolina, those two mad
straniere.

CAROLYN KIZER

TO ARNOLD WITH WHOM I
USED TO PICK RASPBERRIES
WHEN WE WERE CHILDREN
THIRTY-FIVE YEARS AGO

Arnold, you were a fool to shoot yourself:
Social arrangements aren't everything.
Even if your wife threw you out,
Even if your own children turned their backs on
    you,
You should have lived to spite them.
The trouble is you never learned
More than the human species matters.
Now I'll pick for myself the raspberries that you
    can't pick.
The reddest ones are just as good as last year's.

HILDA MADER WILCOX

THE BABYSITTERS

It is ten years, now, since we rowed to Children's
 Island.
The sun flamed straight down that noon on the
 water off Marblehead.
That summer we wore black glasses to hide our
 eyes.
We were always crying, in our spare rooms, little
 put-upon sisters,
In the two, huge, white, handsome houses in
 Swampscott.
When the sweetheart from England appeared,
 with her cream skin and Yardley cosmetics,
I had to sleep in the same room with the baby on
 a too-short cot,
And the seven-year-old wouldn't go out unless his
 jersey stripes
Matched the stripes of his socks.

O it was richness! – eleven rooms and a yacht
With a polished mahogany stair to let into the
 water
And a cabin boy who could decorate cakes in six-
 colored frosting.
But I didn't know how to cook, and babies
 depressed me.
Nights, I wrote in my diary spitefully, my fingers
 red
With triangular scorch marks from ironing tiny
 ruchings and puffed sleeves.
When the sporty wife and her doctor husband
 went on one of their cruises

They left me a borrowed maid named Ellen, "for
  protection,"
And a small Dalmatian.

In your house, the main house, you were better
  off.
You had a rose garden and a guest cottage and a
  model apothecary shop
And a cook and a maid, and knew about the key
  to the bourbon.
I remember you playing "Ja-Da" in a pink piqué
  dress
On the game-room piano, when the "big people"
  were out,
And the maid smoked and shot pool under a
  green-shaded lamp.
The cook had one walleye and couldn't sleep, she
  was so nervous.
On trial, from Ireland, she burned batch after
  batch of cookies
Till she was fired.

O what has come over us, my sister!
On that day-off the two of us cried so hard to get
We lifted a sugared ham and a pineapple from
  the grownups' icebox
And rented an old green boat. I rowed. You read
Aloud, cross-legged on the stern seat, from the
  Generation of Vipers.
So we bobbed out to the island. It was deserted –
A gallery of creaking porches and still interiors,

Stopped and awful as a photograph of somebody
    laughing,
But ten years dead.

The bold gulls dove as if they owned it all.
We picked up sticks of driftwood and beat them
    off,
Then stepped down the steep beach shelf and into
    the water.
We kicked and talked. The thick salt kept us up.
I see us floating there yet, inseparable – two cork
    dolls.
What keyhole have we slipped through, what
    door has shut?
The shadows of the grasses inched round like
    hands of a clock,
And from our opposite continents we wave and
    call.
Everything has happened.

SYLVIA PLATH

LOST, NEVER FOUND

"That is the place," said the Astronomer
Leaning from behind Arcturus
In earth's upper sky
"The planet where they lose things,
Where no one can find
Their lost knives, wives, dogs or hogs,
Their money or their lives
Once the desired object vanishes from sight.
I've studied them six million years
Since my promotion to this job.
Look –
All kind of disappearances:
The crew of the *Marie Celeste*
Is only a splinter of the ships
Boats that went out on business or pleasure
Fishermen rich and poor
In canoes, kayaks, junks
Sailors of triremes
Sailors of submarines
(One lies in a valley
In the mountains of the sea)
Lost and never found.
And not only is the sea
Full of men who failed to answer letters
But consider the desert
Where on one occasion two valuable camels
Were wrongly assumed stolen,
The incident started a tribal war
And never their bones seen
Or their lost footsteps found.

Children, too, have been one moment
All at play in the garden
And the next have stepped through
A door of air into the unknown.
Jewellery and keys have a way
Of departing for parts undisclosed
Without a message
Or a forwarding address.
Parcels go through the post
To the same destination
And somewhere there is wealth untold
Of all the money vanished
Out of wallets, banks, safes
From double-audited accounts
Of respectable merchant ventures
And other less respectable;
From the widow's purse
The collection plate
And every national treasury.
Computers have helped
To lose as much
As ever disappeared from the granaries
Of Thebes or Alexandria or Rome.
Then the names, the languages,
Even the very shapes of things
– The wheel was invented six times,
But who knows about the other five?
Brooches too have fallen in the grass
During processions and tea-parties
Cricket balls, golf balls, arrows and spears
Abound in the vanished place.

Manuscripts, vases, and the results of
    examinations
Sometimes a whole dinner service
With the Romanov crest
Or the mark of some potter
Working in a shed near Limoges.
Answers to sums
Have gone from exercise books overnight,
Along with Frisky,
Black and white dog with red collar
Please call Peter Brown.
As for the causes, the feuds,
The important issues of the day
Lost, never found
Under clouds of argument and gunsmoke
Untraceable forever
Even though thirty incidents in Budapest
And two in Vienna, six on an estate
Ten miles from Sarajevo
And eight conversations
Spoken in the Croat language
Have yet to be discovered
In the graveyards of the Somme.
So, too, is the week
Spent on a certain Caribbean island
Where the passionate embrace
Of two mutual strangers
Left behind a nameless son
To start a long tradition
Of unparented offspring.
For children mislay parents
Just as often as the other way around.

The worst is, to my mind,
The friendship that slips through the door
During an idle conversation
Runs down to the bus-station
Buys a one-way ticket
For some unknown location.
And their gods too, their gods
Also disappear from time and mind
Sometimes by force.
Yet every generation wonders
Where dreams come from,
Or those wholly unexpected moments on the road
When the heart flames with sudden gold.

JEAN D'COSTA

WHAT ARE FRIENDS FOR

What are friends for, my mother asks.
A duty undone, visit missed,
casserole unbaked for sick Jane.
Someone has just made her bitter.

Nothing. They are for nothing, friends,
I think. All they do in the end –
they *touch* you. They fill you like music.

ROSELLEN BROWN

BUT YOU, MY DARLING,
SHOULD HAVE MARRIED
THE PRINCE

When we were children, clasping hands,
do you remember that moist circle, play?
How we were dancing and knew only the
    dandelions,
and the earth was livid with dandelions.
I see us now as in a photograph that never was:
hair like soapbubbles spun by nuns, the singing
raucous as starch. Our cries still echo
down the corridors of my ears: we,
rank and weedy, wanting to be old.

There were no secrets then
to prickle our knees.
No one hid in the closet.
Beards were friendly as forests of grass –
how we trembled, pretending to be lost,
caught in the chins of uncles.

We pared apples, made wishes,
and washed in the first dew of May.
Mother went through our laundry
and we didn't mind . . .
but how we wept when our cousin got married.
Home from the army, his six-month mustache
saluted both sides of his face.
Jealous as bridesmaids we watched
as he married the girl. She had apricot hair
and a cameo ring.

Look, now, how he takes her hand.
Never was it like that, picking scabs!
Peaches and morning were right for those two,
not for us, little pickles, fevered in bed, yanking
knots from our furious hair in the dark
and begging to be blonde.
Nights came. Net notching our chests,
thighs sticky, we went to the dances
and put up our hair.
You lost your virginity
in mother's garden
and finally I was kissed.

Now we are older. You are married.
Natashas both, we have grown up.
Those shivery wonderings lit from the street
are over; cousins put away in paper boxes.
Outside, the walnut trees
grow sticky as old tears
and I lie sweating in the dark.
The dusk comes swallow-winged;
the apples rot with wishes.
Where there is no magic, one stays a toad
and we who screamed to know it
know it, and grow old.

KATHLEEN SPIVACK

III

with clown hats on . . .
love

LOVING

When we loved
we didn't love right.

The mornings weren't funny
and we lost too much sleep.

I wish we could do it all again,
with clown hats on.

JANE STEMBRIDGE

EFFORT AT SPEECH BETWEEN
TWO PEOPLE

Speak to me.   Take my hand.   What are you
  now?
I will tell you all.   I will conceal nothing.
When I was three, a little child read a story about
  a rabbit
who died, in the story, and I crawled under a
  chair:
a pink rabbit: it was my birthday, and a
  candle
burnt a sore spot on my finger, and I was told to
  be happy.

Oh, grow to know me.   I am not happy.   I
  will be open:
Now I am thinking of white sails against a sky
  like music,
like glad horns blowing, and birds tilting, and an
  arm about me.
There was one I loved, who wanted to live,
  sailing.

Speak to me.   Take my hand.   What are you
  now?
When I was nine, I was fruitily sentimental,
fluid: and my widowed aunt played Chopin,
and I bent my head on the painted woodwork,
  and wept.
I want now to be close to you.   I would
link the minutes of my days close, somehow, to
  your days.

I am not happy.   I will be open.
I have liked lamps in evening corners, and quiet
  poems.

There has been fear in my life.   Sometimes I
    speculate
On what a tragedy his life was, really.

Take my hand.   Fist my mind in your
    hand.   What are you now?
When I was fourteen, I had dreams of suicide,
and I stood at a steep window, at sunset, hoping
    toward death:
if the light had not melted clouds and plains to
    beauty,
if light had not transformed that day, I would
    have leapt,
I am unhappy.   I am lonely.   Speak to me.
I will be open.   I think he never loved me:
he loved the bright beaches, the little lips of foam
that ride small waves, he loved the veer of gulls:
he said with a gay mouth: I love you.
    Grow to know me.

What are you now?   If we could touch one
    another,
if these our separate entities could come to grips,
clenched like a Chinese puzzle . . . yesterday
I stood in a crowded street that was live with
    people,
and no one spoke a word, and the morning
    shone.
Everyone silent, moving. . . . Take my hand.
    Speak to me.

MURIEL RUKEYSER

BLACK WOMAN

My hair is springy like the forest grasses
That cushion the feet of squirrels –
Crinkled and blown in a south breeze
Like the small leaves of native bushes.

My black eyes are coals burning
Like a low, full, jungle moon
Through the darkness of being.
In a clear pool I see my face,
Know my knowing.

My hands move pianissimo
Over the music of the night:
Gentle birds fluttering through leaves and grasses
They have not always loved,
Nesting, finding home.

Where are my lovers?
Where are my tall, my lovely princes
Dancing in slow grace
Toward knowledge of my beauty?
Where
Are my beautiful
Black men?

NAOMI LONG MADGETT

MILKWEED

Ghost feathers, angel bones, I see them rise
over West Thirteenth Street, unearthly, shining,
tiny Quixotes sailing off to Heaven
right on schedule: it's the end of August.
I'm tired of transcendence. Let's stay home
tonight, just us, let's take the phone off the hook
and drink a peaceable beer on the fire escape.
Across the darkening garden, our lesbian
   neighbor
is watering her terraceful of scraggly geraniums,
the super and his wife are having a salsa party,
and in a little while the moon will rise
over the weary municipal London plane trees,
and the old classical philologist next door
will look up from his lexicon and remember
that even Zeus came down to us for love.
Love, we could do worse than listen to the city
   breathing
on its way to bed tonight while overhead
cold galaxies of milkweed stream and stream.

KATHA POLLITT

WHEN I HEAR YOUR NAME

When I hear your name
I feel a little robbed of it;
it seems unbelievable
that half a dozen letters could say so much.

My compulsion is to blast down every wall with
   your name,
I'd paint it on all the houses,
there wouldn't be a well
I hadn't leaned into
to shout your name there,
nor a stone mountain
where I hadn't uttered
those six separate letters
that are echoed back.

My compulsion is
to teach the birds to sing it,
to teach the fish to drink it,
to teach men that there is nothing
like the madness of repeating your name.

My compulsion is to forget altogether
the other 22 letters, all the numbers,
the books I've read, the poems I've written.
To say hello with your name.
To beg bread with your name.
"She always says the same thing," they'd say
    when they saw me,
and I'd be so proud, so happy, so self-contained.

And I'll go to the other world with your name on
    my tongue,
and all their questions I'll answer with your
    name
– the judges and saints will understand nothing –
God will sentence me to repeating it endlessly
    and forever.

GLORIA FUERTES

(*translated from the Spanish by Ada Long and Philip Levine*)

A MEMORY

The first time he loved me
I felt my legs grow long
like bananas. I became a stork
or a heron. I grew into my body
lying so long on the shelf
like my sister's dress too
big for me.

HILDA MADER WILCOX

SOLITARY OBSERVATION BROUGHT BACK FROM A SOJOURN IN HELL

At midnight tears
Run into your ears.

LOUISE BOGAN

ALLA THA'S AL RIGHT, BUT

Somebody come and carry me into a seven-day
    kiss
I can' use no historic no national no family bliss
I need an absolutely one to one a seven-day kiss

I can read the daily papers
I can even make a speech
But the news is stuff that tapers
down to salt poured in the breach

I been scheming about my people I been
    scheming about sex
I been dreaming about Africa and nightmaring
    Oedipus the Rex
But what I need is quite specific
terrifying rough stuff and terrific

I need an absolutely one to one a seven-day kiss
I can' use no more historic no national no
    bona fide family bliss
Somebody come and carry me into a seven-day
    kiss
Somebody come on
Somebody come on and carry me
over there!

JUNE JORDAN

46

SOUP

*"A rich man's soup – and all
from a few stones."*

Marcia Brown, STONE SOUP

If your heart feels
like a stone
make stone soup of it.
Borrow the parsley
from a younger woman's garden.
Dig up a bunch of rigid carrots.
Your own icebox is full
of the homelier vegetables.
Now cry into the pot.
When he comes home
serve him a steaming bowlful.
Then watch him as he bites
into the stone.

LINDA PASTAN

47

MY LOVE WANTS TO PARK

My love wants to park
in front of your house.

Thank God.
It's been driving me crazy,
going around and around the block.

It's started breaking laws,
obsessively rolls through boulevard stops,
changes lanes without looking back.

It's taken over the transmission,
drops into second
when I try to drive by,
unrolls its own windows.
I had to pull the horn wires
after it learned to "a-uugah"
at the sight of your address.

So just come out here, please.

Please, just look under the hood
and kick the tires.

Try to stay away from the back seat.

ELOISE KLEIN HEALY

RIDING INTO BATTLE, MY HEART ON YOUR LANCE

You're my peach
You're my prince
Pennoned
Gonfaloned
Tietacked
You joust
Mosey along
Astride your
Falcon steed

You're my bee
You're my berry
My cufflinked
Charlemagne
Of traffic jams
And medieval nights
The modern day
Vassal of
Medici me

NAN SOCOLOW

"i don't know how
to play, either."

let's frolic, dear friend
tho we're 30 & bitter
& our faces attest to our pain.
let's dance without music
and laugh without reason;
to hell with the circus they give us.
let's run in the sun
and run in the moon
and run in the light august rain.
i'll chase you upstairs &
you chase me with washcloths
that you used to wipe up the wine.
i love you i love you
let's run & let's frolic!
i love you i love you
let's learn how to play!

ALTA

LYING HERE ALONE

Lying here alone,
So lost in thinking of you
I forgot to comb
My tangled tresses – oh for
Your hand caressing them smooth!

LADY IZUMI SHIKIBU
(*10th century* A.D.)

I LOVE THE WAY
YOU TAKE ME

I love the way you take me
                  long afterwards I'm still yours

       love becoming love becoming love

                  ANNE WALDMAN

AN ANNOUNCEMENT

This is your last warning!
If you continue to ignore me,
If you continue to show no interest
   in learning my name,
If you have not spoken a phrase of some sort to
   me
by the end of next week –
I will stop dreaming about you.
The Great American Novel
now being formulated in my head,
of which you are the central character,
will be terminated!
I've given you ample, fair, silent warning.
I await your actions.

MARY LONG

KEEPING THE WINDOW CLOSED

The last time
I opened the window
the moon got in,

streaked through
between the sill and sash,
and plunged into the mirror.

It stuck there.
Now I cannot get it
out from between
the mercury and the glass.

Look in the mirror
any time of day or night,
and there the moon is,

guarding the absence
of your image
and gloating serenely.

I resent it;
the stars too,
that were stuck behind
the speed of the moon
into the parlor,

where they roosted
on anything and crackled,
flared, went out,
then flared again,

and vanished.
That . . . bothers me.

BARBARA A. HOLLAND

I AM A LIGHT YOU COULD
READ BY

A flame from each finger,
my hands are candelabra,
my hair stands in a torch.
Out of my mouth a long flame hovers.
Can't anyone see, handing me a newspaper?
Can't anyone see, stamping my book overdue?
I walk blazing along Sixth Avenue,
burning gas blue I buy subway tokens,
a bouquet of coals, I cross the bridge.
Invisible I singe strangers and pass.
Now I am on your street.
How your window flickers.
I come bringing my burning body
like an armful of tigerlilies,
like a votive lantern,
like a roomful of tassels and leopards and grapes
for you to come into,
dance in my burning
and we will flare up together like stars
and fall to sleep.

MARGE PIERCY

IV

all those secrets . . .
mothers and
daughters

REBECCA, SWEET-ONE,
LITTLE-ONE

Rebecca, sweet-one, little-one
Siobhain Levy, fur-pie, loveliness,
sweet-face, sleepy head, Becca,
Becalla, lovely-one, loved-one,
sweet-pie, my favorite, my dear
one, nudnik, silly-face, sweetness,
dear-heart, little terror, little
madness, how many messages you
draw for me,
I love you Mommy
Becky, love, love, Becky, Love
I hate you Mommy
dark eyes
dark eyes
all those secrets you
give me
(Don't tell my teacher, they
write it on a form, they
put it in a file for
hundreds to read.)
and I
hot repository of
all your moods
have birthed you
quick and
shocking creature
you run
like a needle
through my life.

SUSAN GRIFFIN

THE SHAWL

Somewhere on Ellis Island
my mother's mother lost the shawl
the women of the town crocheted for her
out of mauves and purples,
old tunes twisted in the strands,
and every plot the slender figures knew
woven, woven in the pattern.

Away from that shawl
my mother's mother had to move,
toward the waiting train, toward Minnesota,
through the smell of gasoline,
through the sycamores
whose leaves clinked down
like foreign coins.
Even when she tripped
over a broken step

she steadied her canvas bag, paid
her money, wrote her name on the form, washed
in communal showers, put on
her skirt with its stubborn hem. When
they opened the wire gate, she bowed
and hoisted the bag higher
to step over the threshold
into the calling distance
where years stretched out
plain as good dirt
and she began to imagine
the calamity and extreme grace
of someone wearing that mauve shawl
till every night in dreams

she chopped it,
burned it, and
when it rose again,
she buried it.

She spent every minute
chasing the furious rooster, dropping
report cards into her apron pocket, bargaining
in zero weather,
forgetting that old grace,

finally carrying
her children's
children on her hip,
while she stirred the soup,

their breath soft as moss,
their tiny feet
stuttering against her.
My feet, my breath.
She bore my mother
like a speck toward me

as I bear you
in this plain dress
towards your own children.
Again and again I try to glimpse
her shawl blazing
mauve and purple
like old regret,
sunset over Ellis Island.

JEANNE MURRAY WALKER

THE FAIREST ONE OF ALL
for Jane

Pirouettes of you are in order.
There ought to be slithers of satin
and diamonds buckled to your ears
and gold ropes cunningly knotted
under your breasts. A series of mirrors
ought to repeat your bare shoulders
while someone quite gravely
sprinkles rosin on the parquet floor
and the orchestra adjusts itself
to one violin's clear A.
Outside the casement windows
a late snow could set about filling
birds' nests, bee cells and the tines
of apple trees. If there are horses
now let them draw troikas
with bells made of brass to speak harshly
and let the middle-aged queen rap
asking her question.
All this ought to befall.

But in fact it does not. It is summer
in a room smelling of oranges and sweat
the upstairs spare room you live in
when you come home to visit.
You stand here ironing among the suitcases
the jodphurs, tampons, ski boots

among the A. A. Milne, the dust-freckled
glass animals and the one-eyed fake bear rug.
Ironing in sunlight you put me
in mind of an aspen in August
all silverbacked leaf hands, slicking
one seam from wrist to shoulder
parting nine pleats with the hot metal nose
and closing them crisp as a lettuce cup.
You stand in an acre of whiteness
a sweet bending tree, a popple
with hands that kiss, smack, fold, tuck.

So far so good, my darling, my fair
first born, your hair black as ebony
your lips red as blood. But let there be
no mistaking how the dark scheme runs.
Too soon all this will befall:
Too soon the huntsman will come.
He will bring me the heart of a wild boar
and I in error will have it salted and cooked
and I in malice will eat it bit by bit
thinking it yours.
And as we both know, at the appropriate moment
I will be consumed by an inexorable fire
as you look on.

MAXINE KUMIN

GOLD BANGLES:
FOR MY INDIAN DAUGHTER

It is twelve years since I first put on
these bangles. Circles
of yellow Indian gold,
they bruised the bones of my hand
as I pulled them on.
I sleep in them: my husband
can tell my mood
from the sound of my bangles
in the dark.

No ornaments, they are
like hair or fingernails part
of my body.
One has a raised design
or spell. The other
is plain, and dented
by my children's teeth.

Daughter, on your wedding day
I will put golden bangles
on your wrists. Gold
to protect you from want
in strangers' houses, and
for beauty; lying down naked
as on the night you were born,
you shall wear upon your dark skin
gold from this distant country
of your birth.

ERIKA MUMFORD

SLEEP, DARLING

I have a small
daughter called
Cleis, who is
like a golden
flower

I wouldn't
take all Croesus'
kingdom with love
thrown in, for her

SAPPHO

*(translated from the
Greek by Mary Barnard)*

THE MOTHER

Of course I love them, they are my children.
That is my daughter and this my son.
And this is my life I give them to please them.
It has never been used. Keep it safe. Pass it on.

ANNE STEVENSON

MONDAY MORNING

Watering the plants, watching
the water stand on dry dirt,
reluctant to settle, to soak
down to the roots, I am looking,
I know, into myself, the way
women do. Into folds of memory,
the soft surprise of revulsion.
Once I walked in on my mother's
bath, hated her breasts swimming
up at me. Now I see my body
is hers – there's no way
to deny it. Men are always
searching for fathers, or losing
their sons, seeing in them
the chance to let their lives
run clear. They want to carve
their names in stone. Women
don't care what they leave –
a wedding ring, the silver
tea set, the right way to iron
a shirt, a voice insistent
as guilt. We use our words
to ward off what we haven't said –
the dream of being barren
ground, hard and flat, rib and
pelvis, everything picked clean.

JUDY KITCHEN

MAMA

She was a basketball player
In the Oklahoma Panhandle, 1916.
Dark-eyed, innocently graceful
In serge bloomers and middy blouse.
Her black-stockinged legs seemed to go on
    forever
Running, jumping: and—she could shoot!
Dead-eye, every time.
Even at seventy-five, heaped in her reclining
    chair,
Half blind and mad as hell,
She managed to sail across the kitchen a cast
    iron skillet
That nearly decapitated Dad.
He probably never moved so fast in his life—
Certainly not the night my sister was born
To Mama alone in bed in the three-room Boston
    apartment.
"Oh, you poor thing," said the geology Ph.D.
And part-time piano tuner, looking for his hat
Before he even started to get the car,
Which was parked six blocks away—
By the time he got back

Mama had her new, unwashed baby,
And she never forgave him for that—or anything
  else;
Settled into a lifetime of nagging and eating.
Last time I saw that flesh was piled on a hospital
  morgue table,
But it wasn't Mama, though it wore her old size-
  40 bathrobe and felt slippers.
No, it was an Oklahoma grasshopper's outgrown
  shell
That had to be dropped off somewhere,
So Mama could go back to playing basketball
Out in the great New West
Where Oklahoma goes on forever—
Where in pure joy she jumps to intercept
  somebody's ball,
Turns, ducks out of reach, bounces it once
And, with that solemn, sure child's gaze,
Takes dead-aim to shoot—
And score the winning basket of the game!

JANET ADKINS

AT A SUMMER HOTEL
for my daughter,
Rose Van Kirk

I am here with my beautiful bountiful downy
  womanful child,
to be soothed by the sea—not roused by these
  roses roving wild!
My girl is gold in the sun and bold in the
  dazzling water;
she drowses on the blond sand, and in the daisy
  fields my daughter
dreams. Uneasy in the drafty shade, I rock on the
  veranda,
reminded of Europa . . . Persephone . . .
  Miranda.

ISABELLA GARDNER

WHAT YOUR MOTHER
TELLS YOU NOW

母が今言ふ事其内に分て来る、

haha ga ima yu-koto
sono uchi ni
wakatte kuru

What your mother tells you
  now
in time
you will come to know.

MITSUYE YAMADA

MOTHERS, DAUGHTERS

Through every night we hate
preparing the next day's
war. She bangs the door.
Her face laps up my own
despair, the sour, brown eyes,
the heavy hair she won't
tie back. She's cruel,
as if my private meanness
found a way to punish us.
We gnaw at each other's
skulls. Give me what's mine.
I'd haul her back, choking
myself in her, herself
in me. There is a book
called *Poisons* on her shelf.
Her room stinks with incense,
animal turds, hamsters
she strokes like silk. They
exercise on the bathroom
floor, and two drop through
the furnace vent. The whole
house smells of the accident,
the hot skins, the small

flesh rotting. Six days
we turn the gas up then
to fry the dead. I'd fry
her head if I could until
she cried love, love me!

All she won't let me do.
Her stringy figure in
the windowed room shares
its thin bones with no one.
Only her shadow on the glass
waits like an older sister.
Now she stalks, leans forward,
concentrates merely on getting
from here to there. Her feet
are bare. I hear her breathe
where I can't get in. If I
break through to her, she will
drive nails into my tongue.

SHIRLEY KAUFMAN

THE PHOTOGRAPH

Black as a crow's wing was what they said
about my mother's hair. Even now,
back home, someone on the street
will stop me to recall my mother, how beautiful
   she was,
first among her sisters.
In the photograph, her hair
is a spill of ink below the white beret,
a swell of dark water. And her eyes as dark,
her chin lifted, that brusque defining posture
she had just begun in her defense.
Seventeen, on her own,
still a shadow in my father's longing – nothing
the camera could record foretold
her restlessness, the years of shrill
unspecified despair, the clear reproach
of *my* life, just beginning.

The horseshoe hung in the neck of the tree sinks
deeper into heartwood every season.
Sometimes, I hear the past
hum in my ear, its cruel perfected music,
as I turn from the stove
or stop to braid my daughter's thick black hair.

ELLEN BRYANT VOIGHT

V

---

nothing is left over . . .
being women

A WOMAN IS BRUSHING

A woman is brushing, brushing her hair.
Cup of coffee, stack of letters
waiting to be mailed. She thinks
of the cat that will soon have kittens,
so young, so ignorant it tries to jump
to tabletops, forgetting its clumsy bulk.
The woman's arm arcs back again and again.
In the mirror she is not as beautiful
as she remembers she once was, is
when she turns her back on silvered glass.
So many letters written, so many cups
of coffee sipped with careful lips.
She will call her sister today, ask again
if any of her nieces wants a kitten
and what color and what sex.
Ninety-nine, one hundred. The brush
goes down, the cup is emptied,
the woman stands to dress
and walk to the letterbox, whistling.
Eleven thousand days have made her life,
five hundred novels, seven thousand poems.
This hour will tuck into her mind
like a curl into a braid, smooth memory
shaping the woman she will be
tomorrow, twenty years from now,
any time she looks into a mirror
or reads about a puzzled cat
small and heavy with young.

KATHARYN MACHAN AAL

from PATCHWORK

Cuttings

The odd pieces
collected slowly over years,
pieces too small
or rich for the usual patterns:
silks and taffetas, red
from a petticoat,
green soft drapery velvet.

Women cut and sewed, and saved
what fell from their cutting.
And everything that family wore,
whatever warmed them,
anything soft under their heads,
was made by women's hands.
Constant, the daily offering
held between their hands.

Out of the usual pattern of days,
this quilt with no pattern,
bright and odd, made
from richer days they saved for
and saved after, cuttings.

Joinings

One night, sleeping alone, I was cold
and I opened my eyes. On the far wall
the colors of the quilt vibrated
through the dark. I wanted it then.
I wanted to be part of its story,

comfort of years before that hard year,
warmth of lives discontinuous with mine,
the odd pieces joined beneath the surface
with tight, invisible stitches.

I thought of the spare bodies of women,
women who made quilts, who slept under them
and died, and I pulled it down
and wrapped it tight around me,
the weight of it pressing me, and I slept.
And sleeping, my breath passed over
the quilt, and the warmth of my body
that had been escaping, rose
and held in the layers of quilt,
And every breath in that pattern,
and every body that slept there, stirred
and slept with me.

What the breaths said was this:
that life outlasts the living,
the goods their makers, while the days
of the making are lost. In each life
what is left over still waits to be used.

But in the life lived strongly, nothing
is left over, there is nothing to look for.
When we find nothing ready-made, when nothing
whole is given, our offering is to join
the impossible, odd pieces, thread by thread
each day for what will serve. Our gift
will be knowing what to leave behind.

CYNTHIA HUNTINGTON

DOLL POEM

doll is sitting in a box
she watches me
with two gray eyes
i take the top off
& look at her
she is wearing rubbers
to keep her feet dry
she is wearing eyeglasses
2 inches thick
she has padding on her soft behind
she is wearing excuses
all over
she is carrying threads
& buttons
she is a good hausfrau
prepared for all necessities
with kleenex
& kotex
& pencils
& lifesavers
& a boy doll with a wedding ring

she has lists as endless as dirt
    a grocery list
    a christmas list
    a wine list
    a list of sins
    a list of movies
    a list of friends
her lists grow up
& eat lbs. of other lists
she is clean clean clean
she is rabbit quick
she copulates with ideas
she is good as gold
she is desirable as a tooth fairy
she is the color of permanent teeth
ask her her name
& turn her over
she says, ma ma

TOI DERRICOTTE

THREE POEMS FOR WOMEN

1
This is a poem for a woman doing dishes.
This is a poem for a woman doing dishes.
It must be repeated.
It must be repeated,
again and again,
again and again,
because the woman doing dishes
because the woman doing dishes
has trouble hearing
has trouble hearing.

2
And this is another poem for a woman
cleaning the floor
who cannot hear at all.
Let us have a moment of silence
for the woman who cleans the floor.

3
And here is one more poem
for the woman at home
with children.
You never see her at night.
Stare at an empty space and imagine her there,
the woman with children
because she cannot be here to speak
for herself,
and listen
to what you think
she might say.

SUSAN GRIFFIN

MARRIAGE WAS A
FOREIGN COUNTRY

I come to be here
because
they say I must
follow my husband

so I come.

My grandmother cried:
you are not cripple
why
to America?

When we land the boat full
of new brides
lean over railing
with wrinkled glossy pictures
they hold inside hand
like this
so excited
down there a dock full of men
they do same thing
hold pictures
look up and down
like this
they find faces to
match pictures.

Your father   I see him on the dock
he come to Japan to marry
and leave me
I was not a picture bride
I only was afraid.

MITSUYE YAMADA

LATE REPORT FROM MISS
HARRIET ROBINSON'S
THIRD GRADE

1. Waynesboro, Pennsylvania, 1948

This is the year we start fractions, learn
to cut a pie in any number of pieces,
but Gloria Creager and I can't figure out
how to divide the new boy in class.
At recess in bad weather we stay inside
and "Skip to My Lou" around the desks.
She and I fight to dance with Bobby Kribbs.
Sometimes she wins, sometimes I do.
She looks like Shirley Temple but I'm clever.
Whenever Miss Robinson has to leave the room,
I'm elected teacher.
In our class picture
Miss Robinson, head cocked like a turkey hen,
keeps an eye on us. Gloria looks at Bobby,
who stares beyond the borders of the print,
his crew cut pale and thick as a puppy's ruff.
Already he's learned to dodge and feint. (His
    father
coaches the football team to loss after loss.)
Perhaps he knows they'll soon be leaving town,
is dreaming his father's early death, the years
he'll play the game, trying to be his father.

And me? I grin, standing beside him, eyes
closed against the flash or maybe already
a poem flutters behind translucent lids.
Over our heads the alphabet unwinds,

tendrils and loops twining around each other
in a script we are just beginning to understand.
This is the year I start to hate Gloria
forever, the year I refuse to wear leggings
anymore. A cold wind strokes my thighs,
lifts my skirt and smooths it back down.

2. Lewisburg, Pennsylvania, 1981

I am abroad in the world, lose track of everyone,
arrive one day in a place that looks like home
to read aloud my poems, my life. Afterwards
someone says, "Were you in Miss Robinson's
    class?"
He doesn't wax his hair these days, but I know
    him.
I've always been sure I would. "Bobby Kribbs!
Are you still unattached?" He shakes his head,
amused, and then, in the brief space of only
thirty-three years, I see he never loved me,
but raised his eyes by accident from
    the spelling book,
whirled past windows, chalk boards, closets,
    dutifully
clutching my sweaty hand.
How loud I sang
so he would hear my voice above the rest.
"This time," Miss Smith, the music teacher, said,

"I want Jane Hess and Barbara West *not*
to sing." Was Freckle West a rival too?
Their names come back: Ronnie Zimmerman,
 who left
a candy bar on my desk each day (I ate it
too) till his mother got her grocery bill
at the end of the month; Truella Werking,
 who lost
a nickel and got us all kept in because
she said we'd stolen it; Alice and Phyllis Rowe,
whom I dismissed as liars because they claimed
they were twins (one was a midget,
 for heaven's sake).

For the first time I think of Harriet Robinson
as a woman about my age. I think of Bobby
walking home after the reading. It's late.
His daughter's room is dark, but a small light
glows by his wife's bed. She has fallen asleep.
Still, she needs to get under the covers. He rubs
her shoulder and whispers, "Gloria, guess what!"

JANE FLANDERS

WASHDAY RECEET

Bild fire in back
yard to het
kettle of rain water.

Set tubs so smoke
won't blow in eyes
if wind is peart.

Shave one hole cake
lie sope
in bilin water.

Sort things.
Make 3 piles, 1 pile
white, 1 pile
cullord, 1 pile
werk briches and rags.

Stur flour in
cold water to smooth
then thin down
with bilin water.

Rub dirty spots
on board, scrub hard,
then bile.
Rub cullord
but don't bile,
jest rench and starch.

Take white things
out of kettle
with broom stick handel,
then rench,
blew,
and starch.

Spred tee towels
on grass.

Hang old rags
on fence.

Pore rench water
in flower bed.

Scrub porch
with hot sopy water.

Turn tubs
upside down.

Go put on cleen dress –
smooth hair
with side combs,
brew cup of tee –
set
and rest
and rock a spell
and count
yore blessins.

ELIZABETH BANSET

THE BRIDE

They strung me up
like a piñata,
    painted – too brightly –
    cow eyes, big lashes;
    red cheeks and lips,
and cheered three times
as they hoisted me above the crowd.

The music began, and they swung me
back and forth.
They cheered
when men came at me
and finally,
when one blow to my belly
broke it open:

    pink printed napkins, a bouquet
    and corsages, blue garters,
    a silk brassiere, white gloves,
    two rings,
    an antique lace veil;
    pieces of cake
    and bridesmaids' shoes,
    and candy for the children,
    enough to feed them all.

KATHLEEN NORRIS

A TURKISH STORY

The rugweaver kept his daughters at home,
    unmarried.
The soft clash of their bangles said *wish for us,*
    wish.

Longing for a son, a handsome agronomist,
for years he worked on a rug that would have no
    errors:
the blue was disappointment, the red was rancor.
His daughters circled their eyes with kohl and
    went to the market,

they stirred pots, singing
a song about a lion asleep under an almond tree.

When he died each married a husband strong as
    the sea.
They danced on the rug and its errors blazed
    like stars.

KATHA POLLITT

ELLA, IN A SQUARE APRON,
ALONG HIGHWAY 80

She's a copperheaded waitress,
tired and sharp-worded, she hides
her bad brown tooth behind a wicked
smile, and flicks her ass
out of habit, to fend off the pass
that passes for affection.
She keeps her mind the way men
keep a knife – keen to strip the game
down to her size. She has a thin spine,
swallows her eggs cold, and tells lies.
She slaps a wet rag at the truck drivers
if they should complain. She understands
the necessity for pain, turns away
the smaller tips, out of pride, and
keeps a flask under the counter. Once,
she shot a lover who misused her child.
Before she got out of jail, the courts had pounced
and given the child away. Like some
    isolated lake,
her flat blue eyes take care of their own stark
bottoms. Her hands are nervous, curled, ready
to scrape.
The common woman is as common
as a rattlesnake.

JUDY GRAHN

MEETING

i find
women can slip
from the pages of a book
just like pressed flowers
they drop singly or in sprays
transparency of queen anne's lace
orange tiger lily tough

and once i found
blooming at the center of a page
flickering through the mediaeval dampness
the odd exquisite
sophonisba anguissola
who painted portraits
who taught men how to paint
when she herself was blind

for a moment
i touch hyacinths   i feel
the brush stroke of petals
on my cheek

MARY WINFREY

WOMAN RAKING UP THE COURAGE TO BE POET

Should I wait
and be found dead
with this whole wad
of knowledge on me?
I'd rather be picked clean
as goose I am,
all innocent of feathers,
and only in my altogether
of prickly gooseflesh
stride out, pop-eyed and shivering,
to face the cackling music
in my own barnyard.

HILDA MADER WILCOX

from THE BITE

What I wear in the morning pleases
me: green shirt, skirt of wine.   I am wrapped

in myself as the smell of night
wraps round my sleep when I sleep

outside.   By the time
I get to the corner

bar, corner store, corner construction
site, I become divine.   I turn

men into swine.   Leave
them behind me whistling, grunting, wild.

OLGA BROUMAS

WEDDING RING POEM

If you wake up
And go about all day
And find your wedding ring

And engagement ring
Asleep in the sheets,
Is it a sign?

If you brush your hair
And small swallows fly out,
Is it a sign?

If you sleep on your back
And find a tiny glass deer
In your belly button,

Curled up;
If your bones turn to gold;
If your lashes

Cover radioactive eyes;
If a nail breaks and splits,
And a tiny thorn

Grows in its place;
If you learn to fly in the dark;
If you wake up

With a green tongue
Speaking Abyssinian and Greek;
If a hummingbird follows you home;

If the moon gets stuck in your tree;
If over your home
There are only red suns,

Is it a sign?
Is it enough?
Is it ever enough?

SUSAN FROMBERG SCHAEFFER

VI

*magic to
mix with time . . .
growing old*

HOW TO BE OLD

It is easy to be young. (Everybody is,
at first.) It is not easy
to be old. It takes time.
Youth is given; age is achieved.
One must work a magic to mix with time
in order to become old.

Youth is given. One must put it away
like a doll in a closet,
take it out and play with it only
on holidays. One must have many dresses
and dress the doll impeccably
(but not to show the doll, to keep it hidden).

It is necessary to adore the doll,
to remember it in the dark on the ordinary
days, and every day congratulate
one's aging face in the mirror.

In time one will be very old.
In time, one's life will be accomplished.
And in time, in time, the doll –
like new, though ancient – will be found.

MAY SWENSON

SURVIVAL

If ever I am an old lady
I want to be an elegant old lady
redolent of pungent essences, like bayberry.

I plan to be lean
with Gothic hands and vein embroidered skin
and prominent eyes that know what most
   things mean.

My great-granddaughters will be wary
of my eyes, my scent, my strange vocabulary.
I shall serve them tea and wafers while I sip
   sherry.

I shall make them mine with trinkets:
handkerchiefs and scarabs, wigs and lockets,
skeletons and seashells.   I shall fill their baskets.

Then they will ask me for my story
and I shall tell them – tell a phantom story
frail as candleberry smoke.   Truer than history.

BARBARA GREENBERG

THE GOOD BROWN HOUSEWIFE

Now that there is no one to remind
to wash their hands,
she washes her own,
leaving the garden dirt
in clots
under her nails,

thinking how much foolish time
she's spent with brooms,
sweeping out the earth
she'll lie in.

NAOMI FEIGELSON CHASE

AMONG WOMEN

What women wander?
Not many. All. A few.
Most would, now & then,
& no wonder.
Some, and I'm one,
Wander sitting still.
My small grandmother
Bought from every peddler
Less for the ribbons and lace
Than for their scent
Of sleep where you will,
Walk out when you want, choose
Your bread and your company.

She warned me, "Have nothing to lose."

She looked fragile but had
High blood, runner's ankles,
Could endure, endure.
She loved her rooted garden, her
Grand children, her once
Wild young man.
Women wander
As best they can.

MARIE PONSOT

THE OLD LADY UNDER
THE FREEWAY

I've come down here to live on a bed of weeds.

Up there are white spaces with curving ceilings,
Harsh wide silver-fitted cars,
Marching squads of freckled-armed men.

My world is depths of green, a water of fern.
No one would guess that a safety hides here
    below,
Secretly jeweled, dropped in this special pocket.

I'm the mad old lady under the ledge. The good
Who fall headlong off the freeway bridge,
I salvage their nail files, pen knives;
I carve my way in with them;
I make a tunnel with green sides.

At night I lie on my back;
The ferns meet over my face like lover's hair.
They nestle my ear. Their words are unsafe.
The words they say are harsh and green.

I'm roasting shreds of leaf, roasting soup in a
    can.
My air is as solid as the inside of a honeydew
    melon.

DIANA O'HEHIR

BEEING

How to be
        quiet,
        busy,
  working the clover.

How to not take out time
        to announce oneself
        but,
        closed in one's own buzz
        and
  saturated with
  yellow dust of one's trade,

How to go on
  working the clover.

HILDA MADER WILCOX

CAROLINE

She wore
her coming death
as gracefully
as if it were a coat
she'd learned to sew.
When it grew cold enough
she'd simply button it
and go.

LINDA PASTAN

AUTUMN

He told his life story to Mrs. Courtly
Who was a widow. 'Let us get married shortly',
He said. 'I am no longer passionate,
But we can have some conversation before it is
    too late.'

STEVIE SMITH

THE BEAN EATERS

They eat beans mostly, this old yellow pair.
Dinner is a casual affair.
Plain chipware on a plain and creaking wood,
Tin flatware.

Two who are Mostly Good.
Two who have lived their day,
But keep on putting on their clothes
And putting things away.

And remembering . . .
Remembering, with twinklings and twinges,
As they lean over the beans in their rented back
  room
  that is full of beads and receipts and dolls
  and cloths, tobacco crumbs, vases and fringes.

GWENDOLYN BROOKS

IN THE TUNNEL OF SUMMERS

Moving from day into day
I don't know how,
eating these plums now
this morning for breakfast,
tasting of childhood's
mouth-pucker tartness,
watching the broad light
seed in the faces,
honey of barley,
gold ocean, grasses,
as the tunnel of summers,
of nothing but summers,
opens again
in my travelling senses.

I am eight and eighteen and eighty
all the Augusts of my day.

Why should I be, I be
more than another? . . .
brown foot in sandal,
burnt palm on flaked clay
flesh under waterfall
baubled in strong spray,
blood on the stubble
of fly-sweet hay . . .
why not my mother's my
grandmother's ankle
hurting as harvest hurts
thistle and animal?
a needle of burning,
why this way or that way?
They are already building the long straw
    cemetery
where my granddaughter's daughter has been
    born and buried.

ANNE STEVENSON

WARNING

When I am an old woman I shall wear purple
With a red hat which doesn't go, and doesn't suit
  me,
And I shall spend my pension on brandy and
  summer gloves
And satin sandals, and say we've no money for
  butter.
I shall sit down on the pavement when I'm tired
And gobble up samples in shops and press alarm
  bells
And run my stick along the public railings
And make up for the sobriety of my youth.
I shall go out in my slippers in the rain
And pick the flowers in other people's gardens
And learn to spit.

You can wear terrible shirts and grow more fat
And eat three pounds of sausages at a go
Or only bread and pickle for a week
And hoard pens and pencils and beermats and
  things in boxes.

But now we must have clothes that keep us dry
And pay the rent and not swear in the street
And set a good example for the children.
We must have friends to dinner and read the
　　papers.

But maybe I ought to practise a little now?
So people who know me are not too shocked and
　　surprised
When suddenly I am old and start to wear
　　purple.

JENNY JOSEPH

MISS ROSIE

When I watch you
wrapped up like garbage
sitting, surrounded by the smell
of too old potato peels
or
when I watch you
in your old man's shoes
with the little toe cut out
sitting, waiting for your mind
like next week's grocery
I say
when I watch you
you wet brown bag of a woman
who used to be the best looking gal in Georgia
used to be called the Georgia Rose
I stand up
through your destruction
I stand up

LUCILLE CLIFTON

VII

thin light on water . . .
beyond being

WE MANAGE MOST WHEN
WE MANAGE SMALL

What things are steadfast? Not the birds.
Not the bride and groom who hurry
in their brevity to reach one another.
The stars do not blow away as we do.
The heavenly things ignite and freeze.
But not as my hair falls before you.
Fragile and momentary, we continue.
Fearing madness in all things huge
and their requiring. Managing as thin light
on water. Managing only greetings
and farewells. We love a little, as the mice
huddle, as the goat leans against my hand.
As the lovers quickening, riding time.
Making safety in the moment. This touching
home goes far. This fishing in the air.

LINDA GREGG

FORETELLING THE FUTURE

It doesn't matter how it is done,
these hints, these whispers:

whether it is some god
blowing through your head
as through a round bone
flute, or bright
stones fallen on the sand

or a charlatan, stringing you
a line with bird gut,

or smoke, or the taut hair
of a dead girl singing.

It doesn't matter what is said

but you can feel
those crystal hands, stroking
the air around your body
till the air glows white

and you are like the moon
seen from the earth, oval and gentle
and filled with light.

The moon seen from the moon
is a different thing.

MARGARET ATWOOD

HOW EVERYTHING HAPPENS
(Based on a Study of the Wave)

                                         happen.
                                     to
                                 up
                         stacking
                     is
            something
When nothing is happening

When it happens
                  something
                         pulls
                             back
                                 not
                                   to
                                     happen.

When   has happened.
       pulling back   stacking up
                  happens

        has happened   stacks up
When it   something   nothing
                  pulls back while

Then nothing is happening.

                                     happens.

                                 and
                         forward
                     pushes
                 up
            stacks
       something
Then

MAY SWENSON

THESE USELESS ARTIFACTS

When the sun dies,
there will be eight
minutes of light:

not enough
to hoard lemons
or bulbs,
gather wood, explain
how the camera
records the slow
explosion of a rose,
pink missiles of petals.

You are not quick enough
to run a mile.
Fast food chains will sell
a hundred burgers,
the chips
will melt and spread
in the oven—

then only dark
(if this is drama
a neighbor will hurl
himself from the window)

after you knock over
the forget-me-nots
after the sirens
and the first car
splinters against the curb
nothing will hush
the small voices

you won't know nail
polish from eye drops
there will be no chance
to set the alarm   the sun
dial paralyzed

if this is judgment
every leaf will stop

AMY LEVIN

MARY ELLEN SOLT

IT IS RAINING ON THE HOUSE
OF ANNE FRANK

It is raining on the house
of Anne Frank
and on the tourists
herded together under the shadow
of their umbrellas,
on the perfectly silent
tourists who would rather be
somewhere else
but who wait here on stairs
so steep they must rise
to some occasion
high in the empty loft,
in the quaint toilet,
in the skeleton
of a kitchen
or on the map –
each of its arrows
a barb of wire –
with all the dates, the expulsions,
the forbidding shapes
of continents.
And across Amsterdam it is raining
on the Van Gogh museum
where we will hurry next
to see how someone else
could find the pure
center of light
within the dark circle
of his demons.

LINDA PASTAN

121

CASSANDRA WITH A TAIL

A cat stretches from one end
of my childhood to the other.
Those winters, by the hearth,
it spun a yarn of smoke into a ball.
At night, it flickered half-moon eyes
in the dark corners of the house.
By day, its tail twirled a signature
on the sky and pawed the air with grace,
gathering in its coat
the electricity of the storm
and smoothing it into glossy fur.
Wise. With cottony steps.

Self-possessed.
Just once she jumped out of her skin.
One peaceful evening
her tail shot up like a bottle brush
and she leapt onto the chandelier
wailing like an ambulance
as if all the voltage in her fur
exploded out in flashing rage.
None of us understood the cat's prophecy.
We hissed at her to calm her down. . . . And
the earthquake nearly flattened the house.
The oracular cat disappeared,
with my childhood, forever.

But her miracle stayed with me.
Tonight, to my surprise,
she crept inside me.
Bristling with shock, I shook
and bounded back from wall to wall
yammering up a piercing cry
to call you wherever you are:
Listen. You have so little time.
Grab what you can,
whatever is dear, whatever you love.
Deep in the belly of the earth
an atomic blast is swelling up,
nurtured by electronic brains,
and produced by pulsing robots.
This green careening planet
spins blindly in the dark
so close to annihilation.
Listen. *No one listens.* Meow.

BLAGA DIMITROVA

(*translated from Bulgarian by John Balaban*)

PLEASE

Please.
I'm going to ask you
one thing

don't bring on
the future yet,
there is a moment
I need to return to

a moment that lives
in a valley between
our breath
and our breathing.

each time we take in air
it sends another telegram
to memory
to remind us
that it is there
where it was not yesterday –

between us, a moment
has been inhabited by birds
whose wings are sheet lightning
coming down from countries
where we have never been,

on the other side of each other's skin
and within a storm of a different kind,
one more time, let me ask you
for a moment
based on invisible birds

please.
bring them to me
lay them down
here inside
there is always one moment
we need to return to
and everything with wings
is headed there.

COLE SWENSEN

ACKNOWLEDGMENTS

"The Girl in the Garden" by Alejandra Pizarnik. Translated by Alina Rivero. Reprinted by permission of the author.

"Childhood" by Maura Stanton. Poetry Magazine: August 1982. Reprinted by permission of the University of Utah Press.

"I Am Rose" by Gertrude Stein from THE WORLD IS ROUND. Reprinted by permission of Arion Press.

"Charlotte's Web" by Patricia Hampl. Reprinted by permission of the author.

"Liddy's Orange" from THE COLD GELL by Sharon Olds. Copyright © 1987 by Sharon Olds. Reprinted by permission of Alfred A. Knopf, Inc.

"Summers Ago" from THE LOOKING GLASS by Isabella Gardner. Reprinted by permission of the University of Chicago Press.

"Chronicle" by Mei-Mei Berssenbrugge. Reprinted by permission of the author.

"Working Around Words" by Patricia Farewell. Reprinted by permission of the author.

"Light Years" by Barbara Elovic. Reprinted by permission of the author.

"Spring" from THE PASSION OF LIZZIE BORDEN by Ruth Whitman. Copyright © 1973 by Ruth Whitman. Reprinted by permission of October House, Stonington, Connecticut.

"Good-bye to Never-never Land" by Lee Ann Roripaugh. Reprinted by permission of the author.

"Best Friend" from MIRANDA'S by Lillian Morrison. Copyright © 1967 by Lillian Morrison. Reprinted by permission of the author.

"Emigration" by Eleanor Wilner. Reprinted by permission of the author.

"For Jan, in Bar Maria" by Carolyn Kizer. Copyright © 1964 by Carolyn Kizer. From KNOCK UPON SILENCE. Reprinted by permission of Doubleday, a division of Bantam, Doubleday, Dell Publishing Group, Inc.

"To Arnold with Whom I Used to Pick Raspberries" by Hilda Mader Wilcox. Reprinted by permission of the author.

"The Babysitters" from THE COLLECTED POEMS OF SYLVIA PLATH edited by Ted Hughes. Copyright © 1961 by Ted Hughes. Reprinted by permission of Harper & Row, Publishers, Inc.

"Lost, Never Found" by Jean D'Costa. Reprinted by permission of the author.

"What Are Friends For" by Rosellen Brown. Reprinted by permission of Virginia Barbara Literary Agency, Inc.

129

INDEX OF FIRST LINES

When I was, *14*
When I watch you, *112*
When the sun dies, *118*
When we loved, *37*
When we were children, clasping hands, *32*
Winnie-the-Pooh lives in the magic forest now, *15*

You're my peach, *49*

INDEX OF AUTHORS
AND TITLES